AGRICULTURAL BUSINESS SUCCESS SECRETS

DR. KIMBERLY CARLOS

TABLE OF CONTENT

CHAPTER ONE

The Foundation of Agricultural Success

Agriculture, the timeless art of cultivating and nurturing the land, is not just a profession; it's a way of life that sustains humanity. From the dawn of civilization to the modern age, agriculture has been the backbone of our existence. In an ever-changing world, where technology seems to dictate the rules, the agricultural industry remains steadfast, offering not only sustenance but also the promise of prosperity to those who understand its nuances.

In this first chapter, we delve deep into the bedrock of agricultural success. Agriculture is not a pursuit limited to those with vast swaths of land or generations of farming expertise. It is a dynamic industry, constantly evolving with new challenges and opportunities. By understanding the foundations of agricultural success, one can embark on a journey that nurtures both the soil and the soul.

We will explore the profound importance of agriculture in the contemporary world. Beyond feeding a global population that continues to expand, agriculture plays a pivotal role in environmental sustainability, economic stability, and even cultural preservation. We'll examine how the choices we make in agriculture today have far-reaching consequences for our shared future.

Every successful venture begins with a clear vision. Setting well-defined goals is the cornerstone of any agricultural enterprise. We will discuss the process of articulating your objectives and aligning them with your values and resources. Whether you're a seasoned farmer or a novice entrepreneur, understanding your purpose and direction is crucial for success.

Agriculture is not simply about planting seeds and tending to livestock. To thrive in this industry, one must navigate the complex terrain of markets and consumer preferences. In this section, we explore the importance of market research and industry analysis in understanding demand, supply, and trends in the agricultural sector.

Sustainability has become a buzzword in recent years, but in agriculture, it's more than a trend; it's an imperative. We will discuss the critical principles of sustainable agriculture, emphasizing how stewardship of the land is not just environmentally responsible but also economically viable in the long term.

There's no one-size-fits-all approach to agricultural success. The right business model depends on various factors, including your goals, available resources, and local conditions. We'll explore different agricultural business models, from traditional family farms to high-tech agribusinesses, and help you determine which one aligns with your vision.

The Importance of Agriculture in Today's World

In a world marked by rapid urbanization, technological advances, and the digital age, the importance of agriculture may sometimes be overshadowed. However, agriculture remains the cornerstone of human survival and global stability. Its significance in today's world cannot be overstated, touching every aspect of our lives, from the food on our plates to the economies of nations and the preservation of our environment.

At its core, agriculture is the very foundation of human sustenance. It provides the food we eat, the fibers for our clothing, and many of the raw materials for various industries. With a global population exceeding 7 billion people and still growing, the role of agriculture in feeding the world is paramount. It's not merely about providing sustenance; it's about ensuring food security for billions. The ability to produce a consistent and abundant food supply is essential in preventing hunger, malnutrition, and food-related crises.

Beyond nourishment, agriculture also plays a significant role in economic stability. It is a source of livelihood for millions of people worldwide. In many developing nations, it is the primary occupation, offering a means for families to support themselves. The success of the agricultural sector directly impacts a country's economic growth and social well-being. Furthermore, the agriculture industry encompasses much more than farming alone; it involves transportation, storage, processing, marketing, and distribution, contributing to the global economy on a massive scale.

Agriculture is not just an economic force; it's an environmental steward as well. It's deeply entwined with the health of our planet, as it's responsible for a significant portion of greenhouse gas emissions, water usage, and land utilization. Sustainable agriculture practices have taken center stage in addressing climate change, soil degradation, and resource conservation. As the world grapples with the consequences of climate change, agriculture has become a critical player in adapting to and mitigating these effects.

Moreover, agriculture is essential for preserving cultural diversity and traditions. It is deeply rooted in the heritage of many societies, shaping their way of life and identities. Traditional farming practices, passed down through generations, are a testament to the cultural significance of agriculture. In today's globalized world, preserving these traditions and the biodiversity that accompanies them is paramount.

Agriculture is more than just the cultivation of crops and the rearing of livestock. It is a fundamental pillar of human existence, providing sustenance, economic stability, environmental responsibility, and cultural significance. Its importance in today's world is unquestionable, and as we navigate the challenges of the 21st century, it will continue to be at the forefront of efforts to feed a growing population, promote economic development, and protect our planet.

Recognizing the importance of agriculture is not only a matter of survival but also a pathway toward a more sustainable and harmonious future for all of humanity.

Setting Your Agricultural Business Goals

Goal setting is the compass that guides an agricultural business toward success. It provides a clear sense of direction, purpose, and a roadmap for the future. In the realm of agriculture, where the variables are numerous and the stakes are high, establishing well-defined goals is not just advisable; it's essential.

The Importance of Goal Setting

Agricultural businesses, whether large-scale commercial farms or small family operations, benefit from setting clear and measurable goals. These objectives serve as the foundation for decision-making and planning, ensuring that resources are allocated efficiently and efforts are directed towards achieving desired outcomes.

Defining Your Purpose

The first step in setting agricultural business goals is to define your purpose. What do you want to accomplish with your farming or agribusiness venture? Your purpose might be to increase crop yields, expand your product line, improve sustainability, or enhance profitability. It's important to consider your personal values, the needs of your community, and the broader agricultural industry as you determine your purpose.

Specific and Measurable Goals

Effective goals are specific and measurable. Instead of setting a vague goal like "increase farm profits," specify the target, such as "increase annual net profit by 20% within two years." This clarity provides a clear benchmark for success and enables you to track progress.

Realistic and Achievable

Goals should be realistic and attainable. While it's important to aim high, setting goals that are beyond your means or current capabilities can lead to frustration and disappointment.

Consider your available resources, including finances, labor, and equipment, when establishing your goals. Ensure that they are challenging but within reach.

Timely Goals

Agricultural business goals should also have a timeframe for achievement. For instance, "reduce water usage by 15% in the next growing season" establishes a specific time frame for the goal. This time element helps maintain focus and urgency.

Aligning with Your Values

The goals you set should align with your values and long-term vision for your agricultural business. If sustainability and environmental responsibility are central to your values, your goals may revolve around implementing organic farming practices, reducing chemical use, or promoting biodiversity.

Flexibility and Adaptability

The agricultural industry is subject to a range of variables, including weather conditions, market fluctuations, and pest outbreaks. Therefore, it's important to be flexible and adaptable with your goals. In cases of unexpected challenges, having a contingency plan or adjusting your goals can be a sign of sound business acumen.

Setting agricultural business goals is not a one-time task but an ongoing process. Regularly reassess your goals, track your progress, and make adjustments as needed. Goal setting not only gives purpose to your agricultural endeavors but also keeps you motivated, focused, and forward-thinking. It allows you to navigate the ever-evolving landscape of the agricultural industry with confidence, ensuring that your business remains sustainable, profitable, and aligned with your values and long-term vision.

Market Research and Industry Analysis: Navigating Success in Agriculture

In the dynamic world of agriculture, success hinges on understanding the ever-changing landscape of markets, consumer preferences, and industry trends. Market research and industry analysis are indispensable tools that empower agricultural businesses to make informed decisions, optimize their strategies, and thrive in an increasingly competitive environment.

The Significance of Market Research

Market research is the systematic process of collecting, analyzing, and interpreting data relevant to a specific market or industry. In agriculture, this practice is instrumental in identifying opportunities, gauging demand, and assessing the competitive landscape. Let's delve into why market research is a crucial component of agricultural success.

1. Understanding Consumer Needs

Consumer preferences and needs are subject to change over time. Market research allows agricultural businesses to stay attuned to these shifts, ensuring that their products and services align with what the market desires.

Whether it's organic produce, sustainable farming methods, or value-added products, staying in sync with consumer trends is vital for success.

2. Identifying Market Gaps

Through market research, agricultural entrepreneurs can identify gaps or unmet needs in the market. These gaps represent opportunities for innovation and diversification.

For instance, discovering that there is a demand for locally sourced, specialty crops can inspire a new revenue stream for a farm.

3. Targeted Marketing and Promotion

Market research helps agricultural businesses target their marketing efforts more effectively. By knowing their audience and what appeals to them, farmers and agribusinesses can develop marketing campaigns that resonate with potential customers. This leads to increased brand awareness and sales.

4. Risk Mitigation

Market research can also help mitigate risk. By understanding the market and its potential fluctuations, agricultural businesses can make informed decisions about production volumes, pricing strategies, and resource allocation. This reduces the risk of overproduction or market volatility impacting their profitability.

Industry Analysis in Agriculture

While market research is focused on the external market, industry analysis takes a broader view, examining the overall state of the agricultural sector. It encompasses market research but also delves into regulatory, economic, and technological factors that impact the industry. Here's why industry analysis is pivotal in agriculture:

1. Competitive Landscape

Industry analysis provides insights into the competitive landscape, including the key players, market share, and strategies employed by competitors. This knowledge helps agricultural businesses differentiate themselves and find their niche in the market.

2. Regulatory Compliance

Agriculture is subject to numerous regulations, from food safety standards to environmental regulations. Industry analysis ensures that businesses are aware of and compliant with these rules, minimizing legal risks and ensuring responsible operations.

3. Economic Trends

The agricultural industry is influenced by economic factors like commodity prices, inflation, and government policies. Industry analysis helps businesses stay informed about these economic trends, enabling them to adjust their strategies accordingly.

4. Technology and Innovation

Agriculture is rapidly evolving with technological advancements. Industry analysis keeps businesses up to date with the latest innovations in farming practices, machinery, and sustainability efforts. This knowledge is essential for staying competitive and embracing efficiency.

Market research and industry analysis are not merely options for agricultural businesses; they are vital components of success. These practices empower businesses to adapt to changing market dynamics, make informed decisions, and mitigate risks. In the ever-evolving world of agriculture, staying ahead requires a commitment to continuous research and analysis, ultimately ensuring sustainability, profitability, and a prominent place in the industry.

Sustainable Agriculture Practices: Nurturing the Earth and the Future

Sustainable agriculture practices represent a critical shift in the way we approach farming and food production. In a world facing environmental challenges and a growing global population, these practices offer a path toward harmonizing agricultural productivity with long-term environmental and social well-being. The essence of sustainable agriculture lies in its commitment to preserving natural resources, fostering biodiversity, and ensuring food security for generations to come.

Balancing Productivity and Environmental Stewardship

Sustainable agriculture seeks to strike a balance between maximizing crop yields and minimizing the negative environmental impacts of farming. This balance is achieved through a set of practices that prioritize ecological health. Here are some key elements of sustainable agriculture:

1. Soil Health

The foundation of any sustainable agricultural system is healthy soil. Sustainable practices emphasize the importance of soil conservation, reduced erosion, and organic matter enhancement. Techniques such as crop rotation, cover cropping, and reduced tillage help maintain soil structure, fertility, and microbial diversity.

2. Water Management

Water is a precious resource, and sustainable agriculture focuses on efficient water usage. Practices like drip irrigation, rainwater harvesting, and conservation tillage help reduce water wastage and preserve water quality.

3. Biodiversity

Sustainable agriculture encourages biodiversity, both in and around the farm. By planting cover crops, preserving natural habitats, and minimizing the use of pesticides, farms can support a diverse range of species, from pollinators to beneficial predators.

4. Organic Farming

Organic farming practices are a fundamental component of sustainable agriculture. These methods eliminate synthetic chemicals and genetically modified organisms in favor of natural solutions.

Organic farming fosters soil health, minimizes environmental harm, and produces healthier, chemical-free food.

5. Integrated Pest Management

Sustainable agriculture incorporates integrated pest management (IPM) strategies to minimize the use of chemical pesticides. IPM involves monitoring pests, implementing preventive measures, and using biological controls to manage pest populations.

6. Agroforestry

Agroforestry combines trees or other woody plants with crops or livestock. This approach enhances soil fertility, sequesters carbon, and diversifies farm income.

Economic Viability and Food Security

Sustainability isn't limited to environmental concerns; it's also about economic viability and food security. Sustainable agricultural practices promote financial stability by reducing input costs and enhancing long-term productivity.

This means farmers can continue to grow crops and raise livestock without depleting resources or accruing excessive debt.

Sustainable agriculture also contributes to food security. By ensuring a consistent and diverse food supply, these practices reduce the risk of food shortages and price volatility.

The focus on local, small-scale farming fosters resilience

and self-sufficiency in communities.

Challenges and Future Prospects

While sustainable agriculture practices offer numerous benefits, they are not without challenges. Implementing these practices can be resource-intensive, requiring education, training, and investment. However, the long-term benefits far outweigh the initial costs. Sustainable agriculture is not a one-size-fits-all solution, as practices may vary depending on location, climate, and available resources.

The future of agriculture depends on embracing sustainability. As our world grapples with climate change, environmental degradation, and the need to feed a growing population, sustainable agriculture is not a choice; it is an imperative. It offers a vision of a world where the needs of today do not compromise the needs of tomorrow, where the land, water, and ecosystems are preserved, and where food security and economic viability go hand in hand. In sustainable agriculture, we find a model for nurturing the earth and securing a bountiful future for all.

Choosing the Right Agricultural Business Model: A Path to Success

Selecting the appropriate agricultural business model is a pivotal decision that can shape the trajectory of your farming enterprise. From traditional family farms to high-tech agribusiness ventures, the agricultural sector offers a wide array of options. To maximize your chances of success, it's essential to choose a model that aligns with your resources, goals, and local conditions.

Understanding Agricultural Business Models

Agricultural business models encompass a diverse range of approaches, each with its own advantages and challenges. It's vital to consider these models and their unique characteristics before making a choice.

1. Family Farming

Family farming represents the traditional and time-tested model of agriculture. It's often characterized by small- to medium-sized operations, primarily managed and operated by family members. This model fosters a close connection to the land, a focus on sustainability, and the preservation of

24

generational agricultural practices.

2. Commercial Farming

Commercial farming is typically associated with larger-scale, profit-driven operations. These farms often produce a single commodity, such as corn, soybeans, or wheat, and rely on mechanization, economies of scale, and efficient management to maximize yields and profits.

3. Organic Farming

Organic farming focuses on producing crops and livestock without synthetic chemicals or genetically modified organisms. This model is driven by consumer demand for healthy, sustainable, and environmentally friendly products.

4. Specialty Crop Farming

Specialty crop farming centers on the cultivation of unique or high-value crops, such as fruits, vegetables, herbs, or specialty grains. These crops often command premium prices and can be a profitable niche for smaller operations.

5. Livestock Farming

Livestock farming revolves around the raising of animals for meat, dairy, or other products. It includes models like cattle ranching, poultry farming, and dairy operations, each with its own unique demands and opportunities.

6. Agribusiness and Value-Added Products

Agribusiness involves a wide array of activities beyond farming itself, such as food processing, distribution, and retail. Value-added products, such as artisanal cheese or canned goods, transform raw agricultural materials into higher-value goods.

7. Sustainable Farming

Sustainable farming prioritizes environmentally responsible and socially equitable practices. It integrates sustainable agriculture techniques, such as organic farming and conservation practices, into business operations.

Selecting the Right Model

Choosing the right agricultural business model should be a well-informed decision based on several key considerations:

1. Your Resources: Assess the resources you have at your disposal, including land, capital, equipment, and labor.

The model you choose should align with your available resources.

2. Market Demand: Consider the local and global market demand for your chosen agricultural products. Select a model that can cater to these demands effectively.

3. Personal Goals: Define your personal and business goals. Whether you aim to prioritize sustainability, maximize profits, or create a unique brand, your goals should guide your model selection.

Local Conditions: Recognize the environmental, climatic, and regulatory conditions in your region. Different models may be more or less suited to your specific location.

Your Expertise: Be honest about your knowledge and experience in agriculture. If you're new to farming, you may want to start with a simpler model or seek training and education.

Flexibility: Keep in mind that the agricultural business landscape is dynamic. Be prepared to adapt your model as circumstances change.

The right agricultural business model is not a one-size-fits-all solution. It is a reflection of your unique resources, goals, and local conditions.

By thoroughly researching, assessing, and aligning your choice with these factors, you can set the stage for a successful agricultural venture.

Remember that the choice of your business model is not static; it can evolve and grow with your experience, expanding your horizons in the world of agriculture.

CHAPTER TWO

Cultivating Profitable Crops and Livestock: Nurturing the Heart of Agriculture

Agriculture, an age-old practice intricately woven into the fabric of human existence, is not just about tilling the land and rearing animals. It's a dynamic, multifaceted field that serves as the backbone of our food supply, clothing, and numerous other industries. Within this expansive realm, the cultivation of profitable crops and livestock stands as a cornerstone of agricultural success. In this chapter, we embark on a journey into the heart of agriculture, exploring the art and science of growing crops and raising animals with an eye on profitability.

The very essence of agriculture revolves around cultivating crops, a practice that has evolved over centuries into a sophisticated science. This section begins by exploring the fundamental aspect of crop selection. Choosing the right crops is akin to selecting the building blocks of your agricultural enterprise. We'll delve into the criteria that inform these decisions, including local climate, soil quality, market demand, and the specific goals of your agricultural venture.

Crop management, the art of nurturing these chosen plants, is equally crucial. From planting and soil preparation to pest control and irrigation, every step is essential for optimizing yield and quality. Sustainable farming practices, organic cultivation, and innovative techniques all play a role in enhancing crop management. In this section, we'll guide you through the process of growing healthy, robust crops that not only fulfill market demand but also promote long-term sustainability.

Livestock rearing is another integral facet of agriculture, providing a source of sustenance, livelihood, and, when managed effectively, profit. This section ventures into the world of animal husbandry, where choices in breeds, feeding, and animal health profoundly impact the success of your agricultural enterprise.

Selecting the right livestock breeds is an art that requires consideration of factors such as local climate, market demand, and specific objectives. We'll explore how different animal breeds offer distinct advantages and challenges, from dairy cattle to poultry and from beef cattle to swine.

Animal care and well-being are paramount in the world of livestock. Healthy animals are not only ethically important but also contribute to higher yields and product quality. We'll delve into best practices for feeding, housing, and disease management, emphasizing the importance of sustainable and humane care.

Beneath the roots of every thriving crop lies the foundation of fertile soil. Soil health and fertilization are the underpinnings of agricultural success. In this section, we'll journey underground to explore the intricacies of nurturing the earth to produce profitable crops.

Soil health is not a passive aspect of agriculture; it requires conscious management. We'll discuss the principles of soil conservation, including practices such as crop rotation, cover cropping, and reduced tillage, which promote soil fertility, structure, and microbial diversity.

Fertilization plays a pivotal role in crop cultivation. Understanding the nutrient needs of different crops and how to provide them through organic or synthetic fertilizers is crucial. Sustainable soil management techniques, such as composting and nutrient cycling, will also take center stage in this section.

Water is life, and in agriculture, it's the elixir that nourishes crops and sustains livestock. Effective irrigation and water management are essential for ensuring optimal crop growth and animal well-being. This section explores the art of harnessing and conserving this vital resource in a manner that promotes both profitability and sustainability.

Irrigation methods vary based on local conditions and crop requirements. From traditional furrow irrigation to modern drip systems, we'll discuss the pros and cons of each approach and guide you in selecting the most suitable method for your agricultural venture.

Water conservation is an increasingly important aspect of agriculture, especially in regions prone to drought. Sustainable water management practices, such as rainwater harvesting and efficient watering techniques, will be highlighted, ensuring that your agricultural endeavors are environmentally responsible.

In the intricate dance of agriculture, pests and diseases often play the role of unwelcome intruders. Effective pest and disease control strategies are critical to safeguarding your crops and livestock, thus ensuring the profitability and long-term sustainability of your agricultural enterprise.

This section delves into the world of integrated pest management (IPM), a holistic approach to controlling pests while minimizing the use of chemical pesticides. We'll discuss the importance of monitoring, preventive measures, and biological controls in managing pest populations.

Disease prevention and management are equally essential when it comes to livestock. We'll explore best practices for maintaining animal health, implementing vaccination programs, and dealing with disease outbreaks, while emphasizing the importance of responsible antibiotic use.

Crop Selection and Management: Nurturing the Seeds of Agricultural Success

In the world of agriculture, the selection and management of crops are among the most critical decisions that a farmer or agricultural business must make. These choices have a profound impact on everything from yield and profit to sustainability and the environment. Crop selection and management represent the very heart of successful farming.

The Art of Crop Selection

Crop selection is a nuanced process that combines science and art, driven by a blend of factors. It's not merely about planting what you like or what is in demand; it's about understanding your environment, market dynamics, and long-term goals.

Local Climate and Soil Conditions

The first consideration in crop selection is the local climate and soil conditions. Different crops thrive under various temperature, moisture, and soil pH conditions. By understanding your region's climate, including temperature, rainfall, and growing season length, you can identify crops that are likely to do well. Soil testing is equally crucial; it helps determine soil pH, nutrient levels, and drainage characteristics.

Market Demand

While it's essential to consider your local climate and soil, it's equally important to assess market demand. Some crops may grow well in your area but may not be in high demand, leading to challenges in selling your harvest.

Research local and regional markets to identify crops that are needed and could offer a good return on investment.

Farm Goals and Resources

Your farm's goals and available resources are vital factors in crop selection. Are you aiming for maximum yield, sustainable farming, or a niche market? Smaller farms might focus on high-value specialty crops, while larger operations may go for high-yield commodity crops. Your available resources, including land size, equipment, and labor, also impact your crop choices.

Sustainable Crop Management

Once you've selected your crops, effective management is essential to optimize yields and quality. Sustainable crop management practices are critical to long-term success. These practices not only ensure profitability but also promote environmental stewardship. Key components of sustainable crop management include:

Crop Rotation

Crop rotation involves planting different crops in the same field in successive seasons. This practice helps break the cycle of pests and diseases, improves soil health, and enhances nutrient cycling. It is a fundamental practice in sustainable agriculture.

Cover Cropping

Cover cropping involves planting specific crops during the off-season to protect and enrich the soil. Cover crops can reduce erosion, improve soil structure, and provide green manure, enhancing the soil's fertility.

Reduced Tillage

Reduced tillage practices, such as no-till or minimum-till, aim to disturb the soil as little as possible. This conserves moisture, minimizes soil erosion, and helps sequester carbon, promoting environmental sustainability.

Pest and Disease Management

Sustainable pest and disease management focus on minimizing the use of synthetic pesticides. Integrated pest management (IPM) combines biological controls, monitoring, and preventive measures to manage pests effectively while minimizing environmental harm.

Organic Farming

Organic farming is another facet of sustainable crop management. It emphasizes the use of organic matter, compost, and natural inputs to nourish the soil and reduce reliance on synthetic chemicals.

Crop selection and management represent the foundation of a successful farming enterprise. The art of choosing the right crops, informed by local conditions and market demand, sets the stage for profitability.

Sustainable crop management practices, rooted in environmental responsibility, ensure the longevity and ecological health of your farm. It's a delicate balance of science and art, where knowledge, experience, and a deep connection to the land all play a crucial role in nurturing the seeds of agricultural success.

Livestock Rearing and Care: Nurturing the Heart of Agriculture

In the intricate tapestry of agriculture, livestock rearing takes center stage as a vital component. This practice not only sustains human life through the provision of meat, milk, and other products but also plays a pivotal role in enhancing the economic stability of farming operations.

To cultivate profitable and sustainable livestock ventures, it is essential to understand the art and science of livestock rearing and care.

Choosing the Right Livestock

The journey begins with choosing the right livestock, a decision that can shape the future of your agricultural enterprise. Selection encompasses various factors, each of which contributes to the success of your livestock operation:

1. Local Conditions: Understanding your local environment, including climate, soil, and vegetation, is essential for selecting the appropriate livestock breeds. Some breeds thrive in specific climates and terrains, while others may struggle.

2. Market Demand: As with crops, assessing market demand is crucial when selecting livestock. Different regions may have varying preferences for meat, dairy, or other livestock products. Ensuring that your chosen livestock aligns with local demand can lead to better economic outcomes.

3. Your Expertise: Your knowledge and experience with particular livestock species play a significant role in selection. If you have prior experience with cattle, for example, it may be a more natural choice for you than venturing into a new species.

4. Ethical Considerations: Ethical factors, such as animal welfare and sustainable practices, should also guide your choices. Understanding the responsibilities that come with livestock rearing is integral to humane and sustainable farming.

Feeding and Nutrition

Once you've selected your livestock, proper feeding and nutrition are vital to ensure their health, productivity, and the quality of the products they yield. Effective practices in this area include:

1. Balanced Diet: Providing a balanced diet that meets the nutritional needs of your livestock is essential. It's crucial to understand the dietary requirements of your specific species, including their need for proteins, carbohydrates, vitamins, and minerals.

2. Forage and Pasture Management: Grazing and pasture management are essential for ruminants like cattle and sheep. Ensuring that your livestock have access to high-quality forage and maintaining pastures are key aspects of their nutrition.

3. Feed Quality: The quality of the feed you provide, whether it's fresh pasture, hay, grains, or commercial feeds, affects the overall health and productivity of your livestock. Ensuring the feed is free from contaminants and appropriate for the species is crucial.

4. Hydration: Access to clean and abundant water is fundamental to livestock well-being. Proper hydration is essential for digestion, thermoregulation, and overall health.

Disease Prevention and Health Management

Animal health is a top priority in livestock rearing. Disease prevention and health management are critical components of responsible livestock care:

1. Vaccination: Implementing vaccination programs based on the specific diseases prevalent in your region is key to disease prevention. Vaccines help protect your livestock from common illnesses.

2. Disease Monitoring: Regular monitoring for signs of illness or disease is essential. Early detection and prompt treatment can prevent the spread of diseases and minimize economic losses.

3. Responsible Antibiotic Use: The responsible use of antibiotics is vital in livestock health management. Overuse and misuse of antibiotics can lead to antibiotic resistance and harm both animal and human health.

4. Housing and Shelter: Proper housing and shelter protect livestock from harsh weather conditions and provide a comfortable and safe environment. Adequate ventilation, bedding, and space are all essential considerations.

Reproductive Management

Reproductive management is a critical aspect of livestock rearing, ensuring the continuity and growth of your livestock enterprise. It includes strategies for breeding, pregnancy management, and newborn care.

1. Breeding Strategies: Selecting the right breeding strategies, whether through natural mating or artificial insemination, is essential for achieving genetic and productivity goals.

2. Pregnancy and Birth Management: Monitoring pregnancies and ensuring safe and healthy births are fundamental to livestock reproductive management. This includes handling prenatal care and assisting during labor when necessary.

3. Neonatal Care: Caring for newborn animals, including proper colostrum feeding and protection from environmental stressors, is crucial to their survival and long-term health.

Livestock rearing and care represent a complex and multifaceted endeavor within the realm of agriculture. It is a practice that demands a deep understanding of the needs, welfare, and health of the animals in your care.

From selecting the right livestock breeds to ensuring proper nutrition, health management, and reproductive success, responsible and sustainable practices are vital for nurturing both the livestock and the economic viability of your agricultural enterprise.

In this delicate dance between human and animal, the well-being of livestock becomes not only a fundamental agricultural practice but a reflection of our commitment to humane and sustainable farming.

Soil Health and Fertilization: The Bedrock of Agricultural Prosperity

In the intricate world of agriculture, soil health and fertilization stand as the bedrock upon which successful farming enterprises are built. These interlinked practices not only influence crop growth and yield but also have far-reaching implications for environmental sustainability and the world's food security. Understanding the art and science of soil health and fertilization is essential for nurturing fruitful and resilient agricultural systems.

Soil Health: The Foundation of Productive Agriculture

Soil is a dynamic and living entity that serves as the cradle for plant life. Soil health refers to the overall well-being and quality of the soil. A healthy soil ecosystem promotes optimal plant growth by providing a conducive environment for roots, water, nutrients, and beneficial microorganisms. Several key aspects contribute to soil health:

1. Soil Structure: Good soil structure allows for proper aeration, root penetration, and water infiltration. Well-structured soils resist erosion and compaction, fostering ideal conditions for plant growth.

2. Nutrient Availability: Soil serves as the primary reservoir of essential plant nutrients, including nitrogen, phosphorus, and potassium. A healthy soil provides a steady supply of these nutrients to plants, promoting robust growth and higher yields.

3. Microbial Diversity: The presence of a diverse range of microorganisms, such as bacteria and fungi, contributes to nutrient cycling and soil fertility. Healthy soil supports this microbial diversity, ensuring that nutrients are readily available to plants.

4. Organic Matter: The organic matter content of soil significantly influences its health. Organic matter, in the form of decomposed plant and animal material, enhances soil structure, water-holding capacity, and nutrient retention.

5. Soil pH: Soil pH levels affect nutrient availability. A balanced pH is crucial for ensuring that essential nutrients are accessible to plants.

Different crops have varying pH preferences, and soil amendments may be necessary to adjust pH levels.

Fertilization: Nourishing the Earth for Prosperous Crops

Fertilization is the practice of supplementing the soil with essential nutrients to promote plant growth and optimize crop yield.

Understanding the role of fertilization and choosing the right type and timing is fundamental to responsible agriculture. Key aspects of fertilization include:

1. Nutrient Analysis: Before applying fertilizers, it's essential to conduct a nutrient analysis of the soil. Soil testing reveals nutrient deficiencies or imbalances, helping farmers determine which nutrients to supplement and in what quantities.

2. Synthetic and Organic Fertilizers: Fertilizers come in various forms, including synthetic (chemical) and organic (natural) options. Synthetic fertilizers provide nutrients in a concentrated form, while organic fertilizers, like compost and manure, release nutrients slowly over time, improving soil structure and microbial activity.

3. Nitrogen, Phosphorus, and Potassium (N-P-K): The three primary macronutrients for plants are nitrogen (N), phosphorus (P), and potassium (K). Fertilizers are formulated with different ratios of these nutrients, depending on the needs of specific crops and soil conditions.

4. Fertilization Timing: The timing of fertilizer application is essential. It should align with the specific growth stages of the crop to ensure that nutrients are available when plants require them the most.

5. Fertilization Practices: The method of fertilizer application, whether broadcast, banding, or foliar spraying, should be chosen based on the specific crop and the nutrient requirements.

Sustainable Soil Management and Fertilization

Promoting sustainable soil management and fertilization practices is a central concern in modern agriculture. Sustainable agriculture aims to optimize crop productivity while minimizing environmental impacts.

Several strategies support sustainable soil and nutrient management:

1. Crop Rotation: Crop rotation diversifies the types of crops grown on the same land, reducing the risk of soil degradation and nutrient imbalances.

2. Cover Cropping: Cover crops, planted between cash crops, help protect and improve soil health by adding organic matter, reducing erosion, and promoting microbial activity.

3. Reduced Tillage: Reduced tillage practices, such as no-till and minimum-till, minimize soil disturbance, improve water retention, and enhance soil health.

4. Organic Fertilizers: Organic fertilizers, like compost and manure, improve soil structure and microbial diversity, promoting long-term sustainability.

Soil health and fertilization are the linchpins of agricultural prosperity. A well-nourished and healthy soil ecosystem is essential for optimizing crop growth and yield, ensuring the availability of essential plant nutrients, and fostering environmental sustainability. Responsible soil management and fertilization practices not only nourish the Earth but also play a critical role in securing the world's food supply and mitigating the environmental impact of agriculture. In the delicate balance between human intervention and the natural world, soil health and fertilization are fundamental practices that nurture fruitful and resilient agricultural systems.

Irrigation and Water Management: Sustaining Life in Agriculture

Water is the lifeblood of agriculture, an essential resource that nurtures crops, sustains livestock, and ensures the well-being of our planet. Effective irrigation and water management are vital components of successful and sustainable farming practices. In this chapter, we explore the art and science of harnessing this precious resource to optimize crop growth, safeguard livestock, and foster responsible environmental stewardship.

The Importance of Irrigation

In agriculture, irrigation is the practice of supplying controlled amounts of water to soil to facilitate crop growth when natural rainfall is insufficient or unpredictable. The significance of irrigation lies in its capacity to:

- **Mitigate Drought Risks:** By providing water when needed, irrigation helps protect crops from drought conditions.

This is particularly crucial in regions where irregular or insufficient rainfall is common.

- Enhance Crop Yields: Irrigation allows farmers to grow multiple crops throughout the year or cultivate crops that might not thrive without a consistent water supply. This can lead to increased yields and economic stability. Improve Food Security: Reliable irrigation contributes to food security by ensuring a consistent supply of crops, reducing the risk of shortages, and stabilizing food prices.

Diverse Irrigation Methods

Several irrigation methods cater to different farming environments and crop requirements. Key irrigation methods include:

- Surface Irrigation: This traditional method involves flooding or channeling water over the field's surface. Common techniques include furrow, basin, and border irrigation.

- Drip Irrigation: Drip systems deliver water directly to the base of plants through a network of tubes and emitters. This method is highly efficient, conserving water and reducing the risk of disease.

- **Sprinkler Irrigation:** Sprinklers distribute water in the form of raindrops, similar to natural rainfall. This method is widely used for lawns, vegetables, and field crops.

- **Subsurface Irrigation:** Subsurface systems deliver water below the soil surface through buried pipes or tubes. This method reduces water loss due to evaporation.

Water Management and Conservation

Responsible water management in agriculture is critical, as it addresses both water conservation and environmental sustainability. Sustainable practices include:

- **Rainwater Harvesting:** Collecting and storing rainwater for irrigation can supplement water sources, reduce water costs, and alleviate stress on local water systems.

- **Efficient Watering Techniques:** Implementing efficient irrigation scheduling and technology helps minimize water wastage. Monitoring tools and weather data can inform precise irrigation timing and volume.

- **Soil Moisture Monitoring:** Soil moisture sensors enable farmers to determine when and how much to irrigate, preventing overwatering and conserving resources.

- **Water Recycling:** In areas with limited water resources, recycling and reusing irrigation water can be essential. Proper filtration and treatment ensure water quality.

- **Drought-Resistant Crop Varieties:** Choosing crop varieties that are more drought-resistant can reduce irrigation needs and save water.

Environmental Responsibility

Balancing agricultural water use with environmental responsibility is a significant challenge. Sustainable water management practices minimize negative impacts, including water pollution, soil degradation, and habitat disruption.

Protecting natural water sources, implementing water-saving technologies, and using eco-friendly irrigation practices all contribute to environmental sustainability.

Irrigation and water management in agriculture are vital components of sustaining life, ensuring food security, and preserving the environment.

Efficient water utilization optimizes crop growth, minimizes drought risks, and enhances economic stability.

By harnessing this precious resource responsibly and adopting sustainable water management practices, farmers contribute to the well-being of their communities, safeguard the future of agriculture, and nurture a planet where water remains a life-giving force for generations to come.

Pest and Disease Control Strategies: Safeguarding Agricultural Prosperity

In the intricate world of agriculture, the battle against pests and diseases is a continuous challenge.

From microscopic pathogens to larger, voracious insects, these unwelcome intruders can wreak havoc on crops and livestock, jeopardizing not only yields but also the economic stability of farming operations.

Effective pest and disease control strategies are essential to safeguarding agricultural prosperity and ensuring food security.

Integrated Pest Management (IPM): A Holistic Approach

Integrated Pest Management (IPM) is a comprehensive, science-based approach to pest and disease control that focuses on minimizing the use of chemical pesticides while optimizing the protection of crops and livestock. Key elements of IPM include:

- **Monitoring and Scouting:** Regular monitoring for pests and diseases involves the use of traps, visual inspections, and the collection of data. This early detection enables informed decision-making.

- **Preventive Measures:** IPM emphasizes preventive actions, such as selecting pest-resistant crops, crop rotation, and promoting biological controls.

- **Biological Control:** Beneficial insects, predators, and parasites can be deployed to manage pest populations naturally. For example, ladybugs can prey on aphids, reducing their numbers.

- **Selective Pesticide Use:** When chemical pesticides are necessary, IPM prioritizes selective and targeted applications. This minimizes harm to non-target species and the environment.

- **Thresholds:** IPM establishes action thresholds, indicating when pest populations reach levels that require intervention. These thresholds are based on economic and ecological considerations.

Responsible Antibiotic Use in Livestock

In the realm of livestock, disease prevention and control are essential for the health and welfare of animals. The responsible use of antibiotics plays a crucial role in managing diseases. Key practices include:

- **Veterinary Guidance:** Antibiotic use in livestock should be guided by veterinarians who can make informed decisions about treatment, dosage, and duration.

- **Disease Prevention:** Disease prevention is an important component of livestock health. Vaccination, biosecurity measures, and proper nutrition can reduce the need for antibiotics.

- **Withdrawal Periods:** Following antibiotic treatment, a withdrawal period ensures that any antibiotic residues in animal products, such as meat and milk, are below safe levels for human consumption.

- Responsible Drug Selection: Choosing antibiotics that are safe for both animals and humans is crucial. Some antibiotics are classified as critically important for human medicine, and their use in livestock should be minimized.

Disease Monitoring and Prevention in Crops

Crops face their own array of diseases, which can decimate yields if left unaddressed. Disease monitoring and prevention strategies include:

- Resistant Crop Varieties: Planting crop varieties that are resistant to specific diseases can significantly reduce the need for chemical treatments.

- Crop Rotation: Rotating crops can break the life cycles of disease-causing organisms. For example, planting a different crop in the same field can prevent the buildup of soilborne pathogens.

- Sanitation: Maintaining clean and disease-free equipment, tools, and planting materials can help prevent the introduction and spread of diseases.

- Early Detection: Early detection through visual inspections and disease monitoring is crucial. Rapid identification of diseases allows for timely action, reducing damage.

- Fungicides and Bactericides: When disease pressure is high, the responsible use of fungicides and bactericides can be essential to disease management.

Environmental Responsibility

Balancing pest and disease control with environmental responsibility is essential. The overuse of pesticides can harm non-target species, pollinators, and water quality.

Sustainable farming practices, such as crop diversification, buffer zones, and the use of pest-resistant crops, contribute to a more environmentally responsible approach.

Pest and disease control strategies are essential to safeguarding agricultural prosperity, ensuring food security, and minimizing the environmental impact of farming. Adopting a holistic approach, such as Integrated Pest Management, can reduce the reliance on chemical pesticides and promote responsible practices.

In livestock management, responsible antibiotic use, disease prevention, and veterinary guidance contribute to animal well-being and food safety.

By nurturing a balance between effective pest and disease control and environmental stewardship, farmers and agricultural professionals help cultivate a sustainable future where agriculture thrives in harmony with nature.

CHAPTER THREE

Efficient Operations and Resource Management: The Cornerstone of Agricultural Success

In the ever-evolving landscape of agriculture, the pursuit of efficient operations and resource management stands as a linchpin of prosperity. The modern agricultural sector is characterized by complexities ranging from fluctuating market demands and evolving technologies to the growing imperative of environmental stewardship. As such, the ability to optimize operations and judiciously manage resources has become a defining factor for success in farming ventures large and small. In this chapter, we embark on a journey to explore how the art and science of efficient operations and resource management serve as the bedrock of agricultural achievement.

The Changing Face of Agriculture

Agriculture, a practice that has been the lifeblood of human civilization for millennia, is now on the cusp of a new era. Advancements in technology, evolving consumer preferences, and global environmental challenges have transformed the agricultural landscape. In this context, efficiency and resource management have become paramount. Farmers and agricultural professionals must harness innovation, data, and time-tested practices to navigate this dynamic terrain.

The Power of Efficiency

Efficient operations in agriculture are a multifaceted endeavor. This efficiency extends from the field to the supply chain, encompassing everything from planting and harvesting crops to processing, distribution, and marketing. The principles of efficiency include:

- **Precision Agriculture:** Precision agriculture leverages technologies such as GPS, sensors, and data analytics to optimize planting, irrigation, fertilization, and pest control. By delivering inputs precisely where and when they are needed, this approach enhances yield, minimizes waste, and reduces environmental impact.

- **Mechanization:** The adoption of modern machinery, from tractors and harvesters to drones and robotic systems, accelerates and simplifies various farming operations, saving time and labor while improving productivity.

- **Automation:** Automation streamlines tasks such as irrigation, sorting, and packaging. It enhances consistency and reduces reliance on manual labor.

- **Inventory and Supply Chain Management:** Efficient operations extend to supply chain management, ensuring that produce reaches the market at the right time and in optimal condition. This minimizes post-harvest losses and maximizes returns.

Resource Management: Balancing Act

Resource management in agriculture is an intricate balancing act that encompasses a range of critical components:

- **Land and Soil:** Effective land use and soil management practices maintain soil health, prevent erosion, and optimize land productivity.

- **Water:** Responsible water management includes efficient irrigation, conservation, and recycling to ensure sustainable access to this vital resource.

- **Nutrients:** Proper nutrient management involves using fertilizers judiciously to enhance soil fertility, reduce nutrient runoff, and minimize environmental harm. Energy: Sustainable energy use and renewable energy sources are integral to reducing the environmental footprint of agriculture.

- **Waste Management:** Managing agricultural waste, such as crop residues and livestock manure, is essential to minimize environmental impact and promote resource recycling.

- **Financial and Human Resources:** Effective financial and human resource management is vital for optimizing profitability and ensuring the well-being of those involved in agricultural operations.

Environmental Stewardship

Efficiency and resource management are not solely about economic gain but also about responsible stewardship of the environment. Sustainable agriculture practices aim to minimize the negative impact of farming on ecosystems, conserve biodiversity, reduce greenhouse gas emissions, and protect natural resources for future generations. This harmonious blend of productivity and environmental responsibility is at the core of efficient agricultural operations and resource management.

Efficient operations and resource management are pivotal to navigating the dynamic and evolving world of agriculture. They enable farmers and agricultural professionals to optimize yields, reduce waste, and promote sustainability. In this chapter, we embark on a comprehensive exploration of how these essential practices shape the modern agricultural landscape, laying the groundwork for prosperous and responsible farming ventures. The art and science of efficient operations and resource management are more than strategies; they are the cornerstones of agricultural success in an era where sustainability and productivity are intricately intertwined.

Farm Equipment and Technology: The Technological Revolution in Agriculture

Agriculture, once defined by traditional manual labor and primitive tools, has undergone a profound transformation thanks to the advent of modern farm equipment and technology. This revolution has redefined the way we cultivate crops, raise livestock, and manage resources, leading to improved efficiency, increased productivity, and greater sustainability. In this chapter, we delve into the dynamic world of farm equipment and technology, exploring how these innovations have become integral to the modern agricultural landscape.

Mechanization: A Game Changer

Mechanization represents a fundamental shift in the agricultural industry, replacing human and animal labor with machinery and automation. The advantages are manifold:

- **Increased Efficiency:** Modern farm machinery, including tractors, combines, and plows, can perform tasks more quickly and accurately than manual labor, allowing for larger-scale operations.

- **Reduced Labor** Demands: Mechanization lessens the physical demands on agricultural workers, making farming more accessible and less strenuous.

- **Precision Farming:** Advanced machinery, equipped with GPS and data analysis tools, enables precision agriculture. It allows for the precise application of inputs like water, fertilizers, and pesticides, optimizing resource use and minimizing waste.

The Role of Automation

Automation, a key component of modern farm technology, encompasses a wide array of innovations that streamline processes and reduce labor requirements:

- **Irrigation Automation:** Automated irrigation systems, such as drip irrigation and pivot systems, can precisely control water distribution, reducing water waste and enhancing crop health.

- **Robotic Farming:** Robots and autonomous vehicles can perform tasks like weeding, harvesting, and sorting, improving efficiency and labor savings.

- **Drone Technology:** Drones equipped with cameras and sensors provide real-time data on crop health, helping farmers make informed decisions about irrigation, pest control, and nutrient application.

- **Livestock Management:** Automation in livestock farming includes systems for feeding, milking, and monitoring animal health.

Data-Driven Farming

The integration of technology and data analysis into agriculture has led to data-driven farming practices:

- **Internet of Things (IoT):** IoT devices, such as soil sensors and weather stations, gather real-time data, enabling farmers to make timely decisions about irrigation, planting, and pest control.

- **Big Data and Analytics:** Advanced analytics tools process vast amounts of data to provide insights into crop performance, resource management, and market trends.

- **Machine Learning and Artificial Intelligence:** Machine learning algorithms can predict disease outbreaks, optimize resource allocation, and enhance yield predictions.

Biotechnology and Genetic Engineering

Biotechnology has had a profound impact on agriculture, with the development of genetically modified organisms (GMOs) and gene-editing technologies:

- Disease and Pest Resistance: GMO crops are engineered to resist pests and diseases, reducing the need for chemical pesticides.

- Improved Nutritional Value: Genetic engineering has the potential to enhance crop nutritional content, benefiting both consumers and food security.

- Drought Resistance: Drought-resistant crops can thrive in water-scarce regions, increasing agricultural sustainability.

Challenges and Ethical Considerations

While farm equipment and technology offer numerous advantages, they also pose challenges and ethical considerations:

- Access and Affordability: Smaller-scale farmers may struggle to afford advanced equipment and technology, leading to potential inequalities in agricultural productivity.

- Environmental Impact: The excessive use of machinery and automation can have negative environmental consequences, such as soil compaction and greenhouse gas emissions.

- **Ethical Concerns:** The use of GMOs and gene editing raises ethical concerns related to safety, biodiversity, and long-term health effects.

Farm equipment and technology have revolutionized agriculture, enhancing efficiency, increasing productivity, and promoting sustainability. This chapter explores the diverse and transformative innovations that have reshaped farming practices, from mechanization and automation to data-driven farming and biotechnology. While these advancements offer tremendous benefits, they also present challenges and ethical dilemmas that must be addressed as agriculture continues to evolve. The technological revolution in agriculture is an ongoing journey, where innovation and responsibility must go hand in hand to ensure a prosperous and sustainable future for the world's food supply.

Labor Management and Training: Nurturing the Human Capital of Agriculture

In the intricate world of agriculture, the importance of labor management and training cannot be overstated. It's the human element that fuels the engine of farming operations, from planting and harvesting to livestock care and resource management. In this chapter, we explore how effectively managing labor resources and providing training opportunities are essential for fostering agricultural success and sustainability.

Labor Management: Maximizing Human Potential

Labor management in agriculture encompasses the strategic allocation of human resources, effective work coordination, and ensuring the well-being of workers. Key principles include:

- Task Allocation: Assigning tasks to workers based on their skills, experience, and abilities is essential for optimizing efficiency.

A skilled worker in crop planting may not be as effective in livestock care, so aligning assignments with competencies is crucial.

- Workforce Scheduling: Properly planning the workforce schedule aligns labor availability with peak operational demands, ensuring that there are enough hands on deck during critical periods like planting and harvest.

- Workplace Safety: Ensuring a safe working environment is paramount. Reducing the risk of accidents and injuries not only protects the well-being of workers but also minimizes disruptions to the operation.

- Employee Engagement: Engaging and motivating workers contributes to increased job satisfaction, productivity, and retention. Recognition, incentives, and feedback mechanisms are valuable tools in this regard.

Training and Skill Development

Agricultural practices are becoming increasingly sophisticated, and ongoing training is essential to keep workers abreast of new technologies and best practices:

- Technical Skills: Training programs cover a range of technical skills, from machinery operation to crop management, animal husbandry, and pest control. Proficiency in these areas is critical for efficient and responsible farming.

- Safety Training: Given the inherent risks in agriculture, safety training is a fundamental component. Workers must be well-versed in safe practices for operating machinery, handling chemicals, and working with livestock.

- **Environmental Stewardship:** Training can also promote responsible environmental practices, including the judicious use of resources and the implementation of sustainable farming methods.

- **Continuing Education:** Agriculture is a field that continually evolves, driven by advancements in technology, genetics, and environmental concerns. Therefore, providing opportunities for continuing education is vital to keep workers updated and adaptable.

Adapting to Technological Changes

As agriculture becomes more technologically driven, workers need to adapt to new tools and systems. Training should include:

- **Digital Literacy:** Familiarity with farm management software, GPS-guided machinery, and data analytics tools is increasingly necessary for modern agriculture.

- **Equipment Operation:** Training workers on the operation of advanced machinery, drones, and automated systems ensures their safe and efficient use.

- **Data Analysis:** As data-driven farming becomes the norm, workers must be trained to analyze and interpret data for decision-making.

-   **Sustainability Practices:** Understanding and implementing sustainable farming practices is a key area for training, as agriculture seeks to minimize its environmental impact.

Promoting Ethical Labor Practices

As agriculture evolves, ethical labor practices are gaining attention, including fair compensation, reasonable working hours, and adherence to labor laws:

- **Fair Compensation:** Workers should receive fair wages that reflect their skills, responsibilities, and the regional cost of living.

- **Working Hours:** Reasonable working hours are essential for ensuring worker well-being, productivity, and safety.

- **Ethical Recruitment:** Ethical recruitment practices, including fair hiring processes and treatment, are central to labor management.

- **Gender Equality:** Promoting gender equality in agricultural labor is essential for inclusivity and diversity in the field.

Labor management and training are the cornerstones of nurturing the human capital of agriculture. In a rapidly evolving industry, ensuring that workers are skilled, safe, and motivated is essential for optimizing efficiency, embracing technological change, and promoting responsible and sustainable farming practices.

Moreover, ethical labor practices uphold the dignity and well-being of those who work to feed the world. The role of labor management and training in agriculture is not just about growing crops and raising livestock but also about cultivating a workforce that embodies the values of innovation, sustainability, and responsibility in the ever-changing landscape of agriculture.

Financial Planning and Budgeting: Sowing the Seeds of Agricultural Success

Financial planning and budgeting in agriculture serve as a roadmap to prosperity and sustainability. These practices are vital for managing resources efficiently, mitigating risks, and achieving long-term goals in an industry where economic stability and responsible resource management are paramount.

We delve into the critical role that financial planning and budgeting play in the agricultural landscape.

The Significance of Financial Planning

In agriculture, financial planning is a process of setting clear objectives, estimating expenses, and determining the financial resources required to meet these goals. Key aspects include:

- **Goal Setting:** Defining specific, measurable, and time-bound goals is the starting point of financial planning. These goals may encompass crop production targets, livestock expansion, infrastructure development, or debt reduction.

- **Risk Assessment:** Identifying and assessing financial risks, such as market fluctuations, extreme weather events, and production uncertainties, is integral to financial planning.

Strategies for mitigating and managing these risks should be incorporated into the plan.

74

- **Resource Allocation:** Efficient allocation of resources, including labor, land, machinery, and capital, is central to the financial planning process. This includes determining how resources will be used and assessing their availability.

- **Cash Flow Management:** Maintaining a healthy cash flow is vital. This involves ensuring that income is timed to meet expenses, preventing cash shortages during critical periods of production.

The Art of Budgeting

Budgeting in agriculture involves creating a financial plan that outlines expected revenues and expenditures for a specified period, often a year. It provides a framework for monitoring financial performance and managing resources effectively:

- **Revenue Projections:** Budgets should estimate revenues based on expected crop yields, livestock sales, and other income sources. Projections should be conservative and take into account market volatility.

- **Expense Estimation:** Expenses should be categorized into fixed and variable costs. Fixed costs, such as mortgage payments or machinery depreciation, remain constant. Variable costs, like seeds and fertilizers, depend on production levels.

- **Monitoring and Control:** A budget serves as a financial roadmap, enabling farmers to compare actual performance with the budgeted figures. Monitoring and control are essential for identifying discrepancies and taking corrective action.

- **Emergency Funds:** Building contingency funds into the budget is prudent. These reserves can cover unexpected expenses, such as machinery repairs or weather-related damage.

Investment and Financing Strategies

Financial planning and budgeting often involve decisions related to investment and financing:

- **Capital Investments:** Decisions regarding the purchase of land, machinery, or infrastructure are crucial for long-term planning. Evaluating the return on investment is essential.

- **Debt Management:** Planning how to acquire and manage debt, including loans for land purchase or capital investments, is a financial consideration. Managing interest rates and repayment schedules is critical.

- **Financial Sustainability:** Ensuring the long-term sustainability of the farm's financial health is a priority. This includes debt reduction strategies and investment in renewable energy or conservation practices that can save costs over time.

Market and Price Risk Management

In an era of volatile markets, managing price and market risks is integral to financial planning:

- **Market Analysis:** Understanding market trends and potential price fluctuations is crucial for planning production and sales strategies.

- **Crop Insurance:** Obtaining crop insurance can protect against production losses due to factors like weather or disease.

- **Diversification:** Diversifying income sources and crops can help spread risk and reduce dependence on a single market or product.

Financial planning and budgeting are the compass and the fuel for the journey of agricultural success. In an industry where economic stability, resource efficiency, and responsible risk management are paramount, these practices provide guidance and structure.

By setting goals, allocating resources, and preparing for financial challenges, farmers and agricultural professionals can nurture prosperity and sustainability, ensuring that agriculture continues to thrive in an ever-evolving and dynamic landscape.

Financial planning and budgeting are not just tools; they are the foundations of a resilient and thriving agricultural enterprise.

Risk Management and Insurance in Agriculture: Navigating Uncertainty

Agriculture is a sector inherently prone to various forms of risk, from unpredictable weather patterns to market volatility. Effective risk management and insurance play a pivotal role in helping farmers and agricultural businesses navigate these uncertainties. In this chapter, we explore the essential practices and tools that mitigate risk and safeguard agricultural prosperity.

Understanding Agricultural Risks

Agricultural operations face a wide spectrum of risks, including:

- Weather Risks: Droughts, floods, storms, and extreme temperatures can devastate crops and livestock.

- Market Risks: Fluctuations in commodity prices and consumer demand can affect the profitability of agricultural products.

- Production Risks: Challenges like pests, diseases, and crop failure can disrupt production.

- Financial Risks: Farming often involves significant financial investments, making it vulnerable to economic downturns and interest rate fluctuations.

- Legal and Regulatory Risks: Compliance with environmental regulations and labor laws can pose legal risks to agricultural businesses.

Risk Management Strategies

Effective risk management strategies in agriculture aim to minimize the impact of adverse events and maintain long-term sustainability:

- **Diversification:** Planting a variety of crops or raising different types of livestock can reduce the impact of production risks. Diversification spreads the risk of one crop failure affecting the entire operation.

- **Insurance:** Agricultural insurance, such as crop insurance and livestock insurance, can provide protection against losses due to weather, pest damage, or disease outbreaks.

- **Savings and Reserves:** Building financial reserves during good years can provide a safety net for challenging times, helping cover unexpected expenses or revenue shortfalls.

- **Risk Assessment:** Conducting thorough risk assessments and developing contingency plans are essential for identifying and managing potential risks.

- **Sustainable Practices:** Implementing environmentally responsible and sustainable agricultural practices can help mitigate regulatory risks and improve long-term resilience.

Crop Insurance

Crop insurance is a critical risk management tool for agricultural producers. It provides protection against yield losses, revenue declines, and natural disasters. Key features include:

- **Coverage Options:** Crop insurance offers various coverage options, including yield-based policies that protect against production losses and revenue-based policies that safeguard against both yield and price fluctuations.

- **Premiums and Subsidies:** Premium costs are typically shared between the government and the producer, making insurance more affordable for farmers.

- **Claims and Payouts:** When a covered loss occurs, farmers can file a claim to receive compensation, helping them recover financially from losses due to adverse events.

- **Risk Evaluation:** Crop insurance providers often employ risk assessment tools to determine coverage levels and premium rates, taking into account historical data and local conditions.

Livestock Insurance

Livestock insurance is designed to protect producers from financial losses resulting from livestock mortality or reduced market value due to disease, accident, or other covered events. This insurance can apply to various types of livestock, including cattle, poultry, and swine.

- **Types of Coverage:** Livestock insurance may provide coverage for individual animals, groups, or herds, depending on the policy.

- **Cause of Loss:** Covered events typically include accidents, disease outbreaks, and extreme weather conditions.

- **Premiums and Deductibles:** Like crop insurance, livestock insurance involves premium payments and deductible levels that determine the extent of coverage.

- **Risk Management:** Livestock insurance is a key tool for managing the financial risks associated with raising animals, which can be exposed to various health and environmental hazards.

Environmental and Liability Insurance

Environmental and liability insurance is crucial for managing the risks associated with environmental damage, pollution, and potential legal disputes. These types of insurance help protect agricultural businesses from the financial consequences of unforeseen events.

- **Environmental Policies:** Coverage may include protection against pollution-related incidents, such as chemical spills, as well as regulatory compliance.

- **Liability Coverage:** Liability insurance can safeguard agricultural operations against lawsuits related to property damage, injuries, or other legal issues.

- **Environmental Responsibility:** Implementing responsible environmental practices and having adequate insurance coverage can minimize risks and protect the farm's financial health.

Risk management and insurance are the anchors that secure agricultural operations against the tumultuous tides of uncertainty. In an industry marked by multiple forms of risk, these practices provide a sense of stability, enabling farmers and agricultural professionals to weather unforeseen challenges. Through diversification, sound risk assessments, and the protection of insurance, agriculture can continue to thrive and contribute to food security while ensuring the long-term sustainability of the land. I

n the delicate dance between nature and industry, risk management and insurance serve as the buffers that help maintain the prosperity of agriculture, despite the unpredictable factors that often come into play.

Sustainable Resource Management in Agriculture: Nurturing the Earth's Bounty for Generations to Come

Sustainable resource management is the bedrock of responsible and prosperous agriculture. It is the practice of conserving, protecting, and optimizing natural resources, ensuring that they remain abundant and productive for future generations.

We explore the critical role that sustainable resource management plays in the agricultural landscape.

Resource Preservation

Agriculture relies on a range of natural resources, including land, water, soil, and biodiversity. Sustainable resource management aims to preserve these vital assets through careful and responsible stewardship.

- **Soil Health:** Soil is the foundation of agriculture. Sustainable practices, such as crop rotation, cover cropping, and reduced tillage, improve soil structure, prevent erosion, and maintain its fertility.

- **Water Conservation:** Responsible water management practices, including efficient irrigation and water recycling, help protect water sources and reduce waste.

- **Biodiversity:** Biodiversity in agricultural ecosystems is essential for pest control, pollination, and overall ecosystem health. Sustainable farming practices preserve natural habitats and encourage biodiversity.

- **Land Stewardship:** Land management involves maintaining natural landscapes, minimizing land degradation, and preserving agricultural land for future use.

Minimizing Environmental Impact

Sustainable resource management strives to minimize the environmental impact of agriculture. This includes reducing greenhouse gas emissions, minimizing pollution, and conserving energy.

- **Conservation Tillage:** Reduced tillage practices can lower greenhouse gas emissions and preserve soil health.

- **Precision Agriculture:** The use of data-driven farming techniques reduces resource waste and minimizes environmental harm.

- **Renewable Energy:** Utilizing renewable energy sources, such as solar and wind power, can reduce the environmental footprint of agriculture.

- **Waste Reduction:** Responsible waste management and recycling practices reduce the negative impact of agricultural operations.

Sustainable Practices

Numerous sustainable practices contribute to responsible resource management:

- **Organic Farming:** Organic practices prioritize natural soil amendments and eschew synthetic pesticides and fertilizers.

- **Agroforestry:** Combining tree and crop production provides a range of environmental benefits, including improved soil health and enhanced biodiversity.

- **Integrated Pest Management (IPM):** IPM combines biological controls, crop rotation, and judicious pesticide use to manage pests responsibly.

- **Conservation Agriculture:** This approach minimizes soil disturbance, maintains permanent soil cover, and utilizes crop rotations, promoting sustainable land management.

Responsible Resource Allocation

Sustainable resource management involves allocating resources efficiently and judiciously. This includes optimizing the use of water, energy, and fertilizers to prevent waste and minimize costs.

- **Precision Irrigation:** Data-driven irrigation methods, such as drip systems and soil moisture sensors, ensure water is applied where and when it is needed, reducing waste.

- **Nutrient Management:** Responsible use of fertilizers, based on soil testing and crop nutrient requirements, reduces nutrient runoff and protects water quality.

- **Energy Efficiency:** Utilizing energy-efficient machinery and practices minimizes energy consumption and costs.

- **Sustainable Land Use:** Proper land use planning and zoning can protect agricultural land from urban sprawl and support responsible resource management.

Long-Term Sustainability

Sustainable resource management is not only about preserving resources for today but also ensuring their availability for future generations. This long-term perspective underlies the essence of sustainability in agriculture.

- **Education and Awareness:** Promoting sustainable practices through education and awareness campaigns encourages the adoption of responsible resource management techniques.

- **Policy and Regulation:** Government policies and regulations can play a pivotal role in promoting sustainable agriculture and protecting natural resources.

- Economic Incentives: Financial incentives, such as subsidies and grants, can encourage farmers to adopt sustainable practices.

Sustainable resource management in agriculture is the key to preserving the earth's bounty and ensuring the continued vitality of the agricultural sector.

Through responsible stewardship of soil, water, and biodiversity, agriculture can continue to provide for the world's growing population without depleting the resources upon which it depends.

Sustainable practices and efficient resource allocation not only safeguard the environment but also enhance the economic viability of farming.

The practices explored in this chapter are not just guidelines; they are the blueprint for a thriving and sustainable agricultural future, where resource management ensures the earth's bounty for generations to come.

CHAPTER FOUR

Marketing and Growth Strategies: Navigating the Agricultural Horizon

In the ever-evolving landscape of agriculture, where the cultivation of crops and the care of livestock are inextricably linked with market dynamics, marketing and growth strategies have become the compass and engine of success. From the small family farm to large commercial enterprises, the pursuit of prosperity in agriculture hinges on not just what is grown but also how it is brought to market and how the operation expands. In this chapter, we embark on a journey through the intertwined realms of marketing and growth strategies that shape the modern agricultural landscape.

The Changing Face of Agricultural Markets

Agricultural markets, once predominantly local or regional, have witnessed a profound transformation. Today, they are interconnected, influenced by global trends, shifting consumer preferences, and dynamic supply chains. The implications of these changes are felt by farmers and agricultural professionals worldwide, necessitating strategic and innovative approaches to marketing.

The Power of Marketing in Agriculture

Marketing is a multifaceted discipline that goes beyond the sale of produce. In agriculture, marketing involves a range of activities, including:

- **Product Positioning:** Understanding where a product fits in the market and how it is perceived is central to success. Marketing helps position products to meet consumer needs and preferences.

- **Market Research:** Gathering data on consumer behavior, market trends, and competitor strategies informs decision-making and product development.

- **Branding and Image:** Building a strong brand and a positive public image can enhance consumer trust and brand loyalty.

- **Pricing Strategies:** Determining the right pricing strategy is essential for profitability and market competitiveness.

- **Distribution and Logistics:** Ensuring products reach the market efficiently, in optimal condition, and at the right time is crucial.

Growth Strategies in Agriculture

Growth in agriculture extends beyond mere expansion; it encompasses diversification, sustainability, and economic stability. Growth strategies include:

- **Diversification:** Expanding the range of crops or livestock produced can spread risk and increase income potential.

- **Sustainable Practices:** Implementing sustainable farming methods, such as organic farming or regenerative agriculture, can lead to growth while promoting responsible resource management.

- **Market Expansion:** Exploring new markets, both domestically and internationally, offers growth opportunities.

- **Technological Adoption:** Leveraging technology, such as precision agriculture, can enhance efficiency, productivity, and growth.

- **Collaboration and Partnerships:** Teaming up with other businesses, whether for joint ventures, co-marketing, or shared resources, can facilitate growth.

Navigating Challenges

Agricultural markets and growth strategies are not without challenges:

- **Market Volatility:** Market prices can be highly volatile, impacting the profitability of agricultural products. Strategies for managing market risk are essential.

- **Regulatory and Environmental Constraints:** Adhering to environmental regulations and managing the associated costs is a growing challenge in agriculture.

- **Consumer Demands:** Meeting changing consumer preferences for sustainably produced, organic, or locally sourced products can require significant adjustments in marketing and production.

- **Access to Resources:** Access to land, capital, labor, and technology can be barriers to growth for many agricultural businesses.

- **Global Competition:** Global markets bring opportunities but also intensify competition.

Farmers must find their niche and cultivate a competitive edge.

The Role of Innovation

In the modern agricultural landscape, innovation plays a pivotal role in marketing and growth strategies. From adopting cutting-edge technologies to developing unique value-added products, innovation is the engine that propels agriculture into the future.

Marketing and growth strategies are the linchpins of agricultural success in a rapidly changing world. In an industry where market dynamics are increasingly influenced by global factors and sustainability concerns, the ability to adapt, diversify, and innovate is vital.

The practices explored in this chapter go beyond business principles; they are the heart and soul of agriculture's continued prosperity and contribution to food security in a complex and interconnected world. Marketing and growth strategies are the compass that guides farmers and agricultural professionals through uncharted waters while fueling the engine of growth, ensuring that the agricultural horizon continues to evolve and thrive.

Developing a Strong Brand Identity: The Cornerstone of Agricultural Success

In the agricultural sector, where the connection between producers and consumers is vital, developing a strong brand identity is a strategic imperative. A compelling brand identity not only distinguishes agricultural products but also conveys a story, sets expectations, and builds trust. In this chapter, we delve into the essential principles and strategies that underpin the creation of a robust brand identity in agriculture.

The Essence of Brand Identity

Brand identity is the essence of what a brand represents, encapsulating its values, mission, and unique characteristics. It encompasses various elements, including:

- **Brand Name:** The name of a brand is the first point of contact for consumers and should be memorable and representative of the brand's identity.

- **Logo:** The logo is a visual symbol that represents the brand, often with distinct colors, fonts, and shapes that convey the brand's personality.

- Messaging: The messaging includes taglines, slogans, and mission statements that communicate the brand's purpose and promise.

- Visual Identity: This consists of design elements, such as packaging, labels, and marketing materials, that convey the brand's visual identity.

- Values and Culture: The brand identity also encompasses the values, culture, and ethical stance of the brand.

The Power of Storytelling

In agriculture, storytelling is a powerful tool for developing a brand identity. Sharing the journey of the farm, the commitment to sustainable practices, the care for animals, or the history of the family behind the brand can create a compelling narrative that resonates with consumers.

- Authenticity: Authentic storytelling that reflects the brand's true values and practices fosters trust and loyalty.

- Connection: Storytelling creates an emotional connection between the brand and consumers, making it more memorable and relatable.

- **Transparency:** Transparent storytelling, including sharing the brand's production methods and sourcing, builds credibility.

- **Differentiation:** Stories that highlight what makes the brand unique set it apart from competitors.

Branding in Agriculture

Agricultural branding involves unique challenges and opportunities:

- **Farm-Based Brands:** Many agricultural brands are closely tied to specific farms or regions, making place-based branding a powerful strategy.

- **Sustainable Farming:** Brands committed to sustainable farming practices can create a unique selling proposition based on ethical and environmental values.

- **Quality Assurance:** Brand identity can include quality assurance, such as organic or non-GMO certifications, to convey product excellence.

- **Producer Stories:** Sharing the stories of the farmers or producers behind the brand can create a personal connection with consumers.

Consistency and Cohesion

Consistency is a key principle of brand identity. It ensures that all brand elements, from the logo to the messaging and product packaging, maintain a cohesive and unified appearance.

- **Visual Consistency:** Keeping visual elements, such as colors and logo usage, consistent across all brand materials and products is essential.

- **Messaging Consistency:** Consistent messaging and brand values across marketing materials, websites, and social media strengthen brand recognition.

- **Product Consistency:** Maintaining the quality and attributes of products is crucial for upholding the brand's reputation.

Customer-Centric Approach

A strong brand identity is not just about defining who the brand is but also about understanding and meeting the needs of the target audience.

A customer-centric approach involves:

- **Market Research:** Understanding consumer preferences and needs through market research is vital for tailoring the brand identity to the audience.

- **Product Development:** Adapting products and services to address consumer demands and expectations.

- **Feedback and Improvement:** Listening to customer feedback and continuously improving the brand based on their input.

Developing a strong brand identity is not just a marketing exercise; it is the foundation of agricultural success. In a sector where trust, transparency, and values hold significant weight, a compelling brand identity distinguishes agricultural products, fosters loyalty, and ensures longevity. The principles explored in this chapter guide agricultural brands through the process of defining who they are, what they stand for, and how they connect with consumers. Brand identity is not merely a logo or a tagline; it is the embodiment of the agricultural enterprise's values and its promise to provide quality products while preserving the environment and enriching the lives of those it serves.

Sales and Distribution Channels in Agriculture: Bringing Farm to Table

In the world of agriculture, the journey from farm to table is a complex and intricate web of activities, with sales and distribution channels playing a central role.

These channels are the pathways through which agricultural products reach consumers, and their effective management is critical to the success of agricultural businesses.

Let's explore the significance of sales and distribution channels in agriculture and the strategies that enable a seamless journey from producer to consumer.

The Evolution of Agricultural Distribution

The distribution of agricultural products has come a long way from local markets and farm stands. Today's agricultural distribution landscape is characterized by diversity and complexity:

- **Local Markets:** Farmers' markets and roadside stands still play a vital role in many communities, offering a direct link between producers and consumers.

- Wholesale Distribution: Wholesale distributors act as intermediaries, purchasing products from farmers and selling them to retailers and foodservice establishments.

- Retail Sales: Supermarkets, grocery stores, and specialty shops are key retail channels that connect agricultural products to consumers.

- E-commerce: The rise of online marketplaces and direct-to-consumer sales has added a new dimension to agricultural distribution.

The Role of Sales and Distribution Channels

Sales and distribution channels in agriculture serve multiple purposes:

- Market Access: They provide access to consumers, enabling farmers to sell their products and generate revenue.

Convenience: Consumers benefit from the convenience of accessing a wide variety of agricultural products through different channels.

Market Efficiency: These channels help optimize the allocation of resources and ensure the smooth flow of products from farm to consumer.

- Supply Chain Management: Managing the supply chain efficiently is vital for ensuring product quality, minimizing waste, and meeting consumer demands.

Strategies for Effective Distribution

Optimizing sales and distribution channels in agriculture requires a strategic approach:

- Market Analysis: Conducting thorough market research to understand consumer preferences and demands helps tailor distribution strategies.

- Distribution Mix: Evaluating the best mix of distribution channels, which may include a combination of local markets, wholesalers, retailers, and e-commerce.

- Branding and Marketing: Creating a strong brand identity and marketing strategy helps attract consumers through various channels.

- Quality Control: Maintaining product quality throughout the distribution process is essential for consumer satisfaction.

- **Technology Integration:** Leveraging technology, such as supply chain management software and e-commerce platforms, can enhance distribution efficiency.

Challenges and Solutions

The sales and distribution of agricultural products are not without challenges:

- **Seasonality:** Many agricultural products are seasonal, requiring strategies for managing supply and demand fluctuations.

- **Perishability:** Perishable goods, such as fruits and vegetables, must be distributed quickly and efficiently to minimize losses.

- **Transportation Costs:** High transportation costs can impact the profitability of agricultural distribution, necessitating cost-effective solutions.

- **Regulatory Compliance:** Meeting food safety and labeling regulations is essential for agricultural businesses.

- **Market Competition:** Fierce competition among producers, distributors, and retailers requires innovative approaches to stand out.

The Future of Agricultural Distribution

The future of agricultural distribution is characterized by evolving consumer preferences, technological advancements, and sustainability concerns:

- **Sustainable Distribution:** There is a growing focus on sustainable distribution practices that minimize environmental impact and promote ethical sourcing.

- **Online Sales:** E-commerce and direct-to-consumer sales are expected to continue growing, reshaping the distribution landscape.

- **Consumer Transparency:** Consumers are increasingly interested in knowing the origin and production methods of the products they purchase, driving a need for transparent distribution.

Sales and distribution channels in agriculture are the arteries that carry the lifeblood of agricultural products to consumers. In a rapidly changing landscape characterized by diverse distribution methods and evolving consumer preferences, effective distribution strategies are essential.

The principles explored in this chapter offer guidance to agricultural businesses seeking to navigate the complexities of distribution while ensuring their products reach the tables of consumers. Sales and distribution channels in agriculture are more than just conduits; they are the bridges that connect farmers and consumers, enabling a mutually beneficial exchange of quality agricultural products that nourish and sustain our communities.

Exporting Agricultural Products: Growing Beyond Borders

Exporting agricultural products is a pivotal strategy for agricultural businesses looking to expand their market reach, diversify revenue streams, and contribute to global food security. In this chapter, we explore the significance of agricultural exports and the strategies that facilitate successful expansion into international markets.

The Global Context of Agricultural Exports

The international agricultural market is vast and diverse, encompassing a wide range of products, from grains and produce to livestock, dairy, and processed goods.

Agricultural exports serve both economic and humanitarian purposes, contributing to food security, rural development, and economic growth.

- **Food Security:** Agricultural exports provide access to diverse food sources for consumers worldwide, helping to alleviate food scarcity and enhance dietary diversity.

- **Economic Growth:** For exporting countries, agricultural exports generate revenue and stimulate economic development, supporting jobs and infrastructure.

- **Global Supply Chains:** Agricultural exports are integral to the global food supply chain, ensuring that consumers have access to a wide variety of products throughout the year.

- **Sustainable Agriculture:** Exporting encourages the adoption of sustainable farming practices, as producers seek to meet international standards and certifications.

Exporting Challenges and Solutions

Exporting agricultural products comes with unique challenges, which can be addressed with the right strategies:

- **Quality Assurance:** Maintaining consistent product quality is essential for success. Implementing quality control measures and adhering to international standards and certifications is vital.

- **Market Research:** Conducting comprehensive market research helps identify target markets, consumer preferences, and competitors, enabling producers to tailor products to meet demand.

- **Transportation and Logistics:** Efficient transportation and logistics are crucial to ensuring that products reach international markets in good condition. Effective cold chain management is particularly important for perishable goods.

- **Regulatory Compliance:** Meeting the legal and regulatory requirements of the destination country is essential. This includes adhering to customs, food safety, and labeling regulations.

- **Currency Exchange and Payment Risks:** Fluctuations in exchange rates and payment risks can affect the profitability of exports. Hedging strategies and secure payment methods can mitigate these risks.

Market Diversification and Product Adaptation

Diversifying export markets and adapting products to meet the specific requirements of each market are fundamental strategies for success:

- **Market Diversification:** Relying on a single export market can be risky. Diversifying into multiple markets helps spread risk and stabilize revenue streams.

- **Product Adaptation:** Tailoring products to meet the preferences and needs of each market is vital. This may involve adjusting packaging, labeling, or product attributes.

- **Specialty and Niche Markets:** Exploring specialty or niche markets, such as organic, non-GMO, or ethically sourced products, can provide a competitive edge.

Export Promotion and Support

Many governments and industry organizations provide support and resources to facilitate agricultural exports:

- **Export Promotion Agencies:** Government agencies and trade promotion organizations offer export assistance, including market research, trade missions, and promotional activities.

- **Financial Support:** Export grants, subsidies, and credit facilities are available to support agricultural businesses in their international expansion efforts.

- **Training and Education:** Exporting often requires knowledge of export documentation, logistics, and international trade regulations. Training and educational programs are valuable resources.

The Future of Agricultural Exports

The future of agricultural exports is characterized by increasing demand for high-quality and sustainable products. Trends include:

- **Sustainability:** Consumers and importers are increasingly focused on sustainable and ethical production, creating opportunities for eco-friendly agricultural products.

- **E-commerce:** The growth of e-commerce platforms is opening new avenues for exporting directly to consumers.

- **Technology:** Advancements in technology, such as blockchain and traceability systems, are enhancing transparency and quality assurance in exports.

Exporting agricultural products is not just a business strategy; it is a vital component of global food security and economic development. In an interconnected world, agricultural exports bring diverse and nutritious products to consumers, support livelihoods in rural communities, and promote sustainable farming practices. The principles explored in this chapter offer guidance to agricultural businesses seeking to venture beyond borders, connecting with international markets, and contributing to the global effort to feed the world. Exporting agricultural products is not just about sending goods abroad; it is about bridging cultures, nurturing global relationships, and ensuring that agriculture continues to be a vital link in the chain of humanity's sustenance.

Scaling Your Agricultural Business: Cultivating Growth

Scaling an agricultural business is a strategic endeavor that involves expanding operations to increase production, revenue, and market reach. Successful scaling requires careful planning, resource management, and adaptability to address the growing demands and opportunities in the agricultural sector. In this chapter, we explore the importance of scaling an agricultural business and the strategies for cultivating growth.

The Imperative of Scaling in Agriculture

Agriculture is not only about sowing and reaping; it's about evolution and adaptation. Scaling is driven by various imperatives:

- **Meeting Growing Demand:** With the world's population on the rise, the demand for agricultural products is increasing. Scaling is necessary to meet this demand.

- **Economic Efficiency:** As agricultural operations grow, they can often achieve economies of scale, reducing production costs and increasing profitability.

- **Market Diversification:** Scaling allows agricultural businesses to diversify their markets, reducing dependency on a single market and spreading risk.

- **Technological Advancements:** Innovations in technology, from precision agriculture to automated farming equipment, enable more efficient and productive farming, facilitating scaling.

Strategies for Scaling Agricultural Business

Scaling agricultural operations necessitates a well-structured approach:

- **Business Plan:** Develop a comprehensive business plan that outlines your growth goals, strategies, and resource requirements. A clear plan serves as a roadmap for expansion.

- **Investment and Financing:** Access to capital is often essential for scaling. Explore funding options such as loans, grants, investors, or reinvested profits.

- **Technology Adoption:** Embrace technology to enhance productivity, optimize resource use, and streamline operations. This may include precision agriculture, data analytics, and automation.

- **Resource Management:** Efficiently manage resources, including land, labor, and equipment. Proper resource allocation is critical to scaling effectively.

- **Market Research:** Thorough market research helps identify growth opportunities, target markets, and consumer demands. Tailor your scaling efforts to meet specific market needs.

Sustainable Scaling

Sustainable scaling involves balancing growth with responsible practices:

- **Environmental Stewardship:** Implement sustainable farming practices to minimize environmental impact and ensure the long-term health of the land.

- **Ethical Considerations:** Maintain ethical and socially responsible practices, including fair labor conditions and responsible sourcing.

- **Quality Assurance:** Ensure that product quality is consistently maintained, even as you expand production.

- **Regulatory Compliance:** Adhere to local and international regulations, particularly when exporting agricultural products.

- **Risk Management:** As operations grow, risk management becomes more critical. Strategies for risk assessment and mitigation are essential.

Challenges and Adaptation

Scaling agricultural businesses often face challenges:

- **Capital Constraints:** Access to funding can be a barrier to scaling. Seek financial solutions that align with your growth plans.

- **Market Volatility:** Market fluctuations can affect profitability. Diversify products and markets to reduce the impact of volatility.

- **Resource Limitations:** Scarcity of land, water, or skilled labor can hinder scaling. Innovative resource management is essential.

- **Competitive Landscape:** As you expand, you may encounter increased competition. Stay agile and differentiate your products and services.

Measuring Success

Success in scaling is not just about growth; it's about

sustainability and profitability. Key performance indicators (KPIs) include increased revenue, reduced production costs, expansion into new markets, and maintaining product quality and consistency.

Scaling an agricultural business is an intricate journey, one that requires vision, adaptability, and resourcefulness. In an ever-evolving agricultural landscape, scaling is not just about expansion; it's about ensuring the sustainability of agriculture and its contribution to food security and economic development.

The principles explored in this chapter serve as a guide for agricultural entrepreneurs and professionals seeking to cultivate growth, increase market reach, and thrive in an evolving agricultural sector.

Scaling an agricultural business is not merely about growing in size; it's about growing in impact, efficiency, and relevance, while sustaining the roots of agriculture's vitality in a dynamic and interconnected world.

Innovations and Emerging Trends in Agriculture: Cultivating the Future

Agriculture is not the same as it was a generation ago. Today, it is a dynamic and ever-evolving industry that thrives on innovation and adaptation.

Emerging trends and innovations in agriculture are revolutionizing the way we produce, manage, and distribute food and agricultural products.

Let's we delve into the exciting world of agriculture's technological and environmental advancements and explore how these innovations are shaping the future of farming.

Precision Agriculture

Precision agriculture is a transformative approach that employs data-driven technologies to optimize farming operations. It allows farmers to make informed decisions, reduce waste, and maximize yields.

- Remote Sensing: Satellite imagery, drones, and sensors collect data on crop health, soil conditions, and pest infestations.

- **Data Analytics:** Advanced analytics and machine learning help farmers interpret data and make decisions, such as when and where to apply fertilizers or irrigation.

- **GPS Technology:** GPS-guided tractors and equipment enable precise planting, cultivating, and harvesting, minimizing overlap and resource use.

Sustainable Farming Practices

Sustainability is a growing concern in agriculture. Innovations in sustainable farming practices aim to preserve the environment, conserve resources, and ensure long-term agricultural viability.

- **Regenerative Agriculture:** Regenerative practices focus on improving soil health, sequestering carbon, and enhancing biodiversity.

- **Organic Farming:** The organic movement continues to grow, emphasizing the use of natural inputs, reduced chemical usage, and soil health.

- **Agroforestry:** Combining tree planting with agriculture improves land use, provides habitat for wildlife, and sequesters carbon.

- Climate-Resilient Crops: Breeders are developing crops that are more resilient to extreme weather conditions, contributing to food security in a changing climate.

Vertical Farming and Urban Agriculture

Vertical farming and urban agriculture are revolutionizing the way we produce food in urban areas. These practices bring farming closer to consumers and reduce the environmental impact of transportation.

- Indoor Vertical Farms: Growing crops in controlled environments, such as vertical farms, uses less water and eliminates exposure to pests and adverse weather conditions.

- Rooftop and Community Gardens: Urban agriculture initiatives enable city residents to grow their food, promoting local food production and sustainability.

Biotechnology and Genetic Engineering

Biotechnology and genetic engineering continue to play a pivotal role in agriculture, offering solutions to various challenges:

- **Genetically Modified Crops:** GMO crops are developed to resist pests, withstand herbicides, and improve nutritional content.

- **Gene Editing:** CRISPR and other gene-editing techniques allow for precise modifications in plant genetics, offering the potential to enhance crop resilience and nutrition.

- **Biofortification:** Biofortified crops are enriched with essential nutrients, addressing malnutrition in vulnerable populations.

Digital Agriculture

Digital agriculture leverages digital tools and platforms to streamline farming practices and provide essential resources to farmers:

- **Farm Management Software:** Software applications help farmers plan, monitor, and optimize their operations.

- **Mobile Apps:** Mobile apps provide real-time weather information, pest identification, and market prices.

- **Blockchain Technology:** Blockchain enables transparent supply chains, allowing consumers to trace the origin of their food.

- E-commerce Platforms: Online marketplaces facilitate direct-to-consumer sales and expand market reach for small-scale farmers.

Future Challenges and Adaptations

As agriculture advances, it faces challenges like resource scarcity, climate change, and global food security. Future adaptations include:

- Water-Saving Technologies: Water-efficient irrigation systems and drought-resistant crops are vital for conserving water.

- Sustainable Packaging: Eco-friendly packaging solutions are crucial to reduce waste in the food supply chain.

- Data Security: Protecting the sensitive data collected through digital agriculture is a growing concern.

- Consumer Awareness: Increasing consumer demand for transparency and sustainability requires farmers and producers to adapt to evolving expectations.

The future of agriculture is vibrant and promising, driven by the relentless pursuit of innovation and sustainability. These emerging trends and innovations are the catalysts for a more efficient, resilient, and environmentally friendly agricultural sector.

In a world grappling with pressing challenges like climate change and food security, these innovations are paving the way for a future where agriculture not only sustains the world but also nurtures the planet.

Agriculture, in its constant transformation, continues to be a beacon of hope for a sustainable and prosperous future.

CONCLUSION

Agricultural Business Success Secrets: Nurturing Prosperity from the Ground Up

Achieving success in the agricultural business is not merely about sowing seeds and reaping the harvest; it's about understanding and navigating the unique challenges and opportunities that this industry presents. Here are some agricultural business success secrets that can guide you on the path to prosperity.

1. Adaptability and Innovation:

One of the most critical secrets to success in agriculture is the ability to adapt to changing circumstances and embrace innovation. The agricultural landscape is constantly evolving due to technological advancements, shifting consumer preferences, and climate variability. Successful agricultural businesses are agile and open to adopting new practices, technologies, and approaches that enhance efficiency and sustainability.

2. Market Awareness:

Knowing your market is essential. Understand consumer trends, demands, and the competitive landscape. Conduct thorough market research to identify opportunities and gaps. Successful agricultural businesses keep a keen eye on market dynamics, ensuring their products align with consumer needs and preferences.

3. Sustainable Practices:

Sustainability is no longer an option; it's a mandate. Implementing sustainable farming practices not only contributes to environmental preservation but also responds to the growing demand for responsibly sourced products. Successful agricultural businesses prioritize sustainability, incorporating practices like organic farming, soil health management, and responsible resource use.

4. Quality Assurance:

Consistency in product quality is the hallmark of successful agricultural businesses. Whether it's fruits, vegetables, livestock, or processed goods, maintaining high-quality standards is non-negotiable. Implement rigorous quality control measures to ensure that your products meet or exceed customer expectations.

5. Financial Prudence:

Agriculture involves inherent risks, from weather-related disasters to market price volatility. Successful agricultural businesses manage these risks through sound financial planning, prudent budgeting, and risk management strategies. Being financially prepared for unforeseen challenges is a secret to weathering storms and ensuring long-term success.

6. Resilience and Perseverance:

Agriculture can be challenging, with unpredictable seasons, pest outbreaks, and unforeseen setbacks. Successful agricultural businesses demonstrate resilience and perseverance. They learn from failures, adapt to challenges, and stay committed to their vision.

7. Knowledge and Education:

Never stop learning. Stay updated with the latest agricultural research, technologies, and best practices. Attending workshops, seminars, and conferences can provide valuable insights and networking opportunities. Successful agricultural businesses invest in knowledge and continuously seek opportunities for improvement.

8. Community Engagement:

Building strong relationships with the local community and industry partners can be a secret to success. Collaborations, support networks, and a positive reputation within the community can offer assistance during tough times and create opportunities for growth.

In the dynamic and interconnected world of agriculture, these success secrets form the foundation for prosperous and sustainable agricultural businesses.

By embracing adaptability, market awareness, sustainability, quality assurance, financial prudence, resilience, education, and community engagement, you can nurture your agricultural venture from the ground up and reap the rewards of your hard work and dedication.

Good Luck in your journey towards agriculture success…